PRICE
DOESN'T MATTER,
PAYMENT
DOES

BY
JULIO C ROQUE

Copyright © 2020 by Julio C Roque

Printed in the United States of America

All rights reserved. No part of this publication may be reproduced, distributed, or transmitted in any form or by any means, including photocopying, recording, or other electronic or mechanical methods without the prior written permission of the publisher, except in the case of brief quotations embodied in critical reviews and certain other non-commercial uses permitted by copyright law.

For permission requests, please contact the publisher using the contact information below.

Published by Roque Enterprise, LLC

Copyright © 2020

For any requests, please contact the publisher

info@pricedoesntmatter.com

All rights reserved

Disclaimer: This book is for educational and informational purposes only. It is not intended to provide any financial, legal, or credit advice. Always be sure to consult with the right professionals before making any decisions.

Contents

Dedication 1
Introduction 3
About The Author 7

CHAPTER 1: TRUE AFFORDABILITY: HOW A MORTGAGE REALLY WORKS! 9

DTI Explained 10
The Truth Behind a Bank Pre-Approval 11
More for Your Money 14
Owner Occupied Investment Property 16

CHAPTER 2: PROPER PLANNING 21

Type of Home 21
Budgeting 24
Credit 26
Co-Signing 28
Required Funds 30

CHAPTER 3: UNDERSTANDING INCOME 35

W2 Income 35
Using Multiple Jobs 36
Commissioned and Variable Income 37
Self-Employed Borrowers 38
Schedule E Rental Income 41
Social Security, Retirement, Child Support, and Foster Care Income 43

CHAPTER 4: LOAN PROGRAMS 45

Overlays 46
FHA 47
Conventional 49
Fannie Mae HomeReady 50
Freddie Mac HomePossible 51

- VA 52
- USDA 52
- Community Grant Programs 53

CHAPTER 5: GETTING A PRE-APPROVAL 57
- The Secret to a Smooth Transaction.. 57
- Organization is the Key 58

CHAPTER 6: THE DREAM TEAM 63
- The Right Team = A Successful Transaction 64

CHAPTER 7: YOUR DREAM HOME AWAITS 69
- Searching for the Right Home... 69
- Bidding Wars and Negotiating an Offer 72
- Important Offer Dates... 77
- Home and Other Inspections 81
- Negotiating Inspection Results 81
- The Purchase and Sales Agreement... 82

CHAPTER 8: SECURING FINANCING 85
- Required Documents... 85
- Motivation Letters and Letters of Explanation 87
- Getting Insurance... 90
- The Appraisal 90
- The Wait 91

CHAPTER 9: CLEARED TO CLOSE & THE CLOSING 93
- CTC "Music to My Ears" 93
- The Closing.. 94

CHAPTER 10: POST-CLOSING 97
- Utilities... 97
- Check Your Windows... 98
- Outdoor Water Faucets and Hoses 98
- Look for Cracks 98
- Filters and Heating 98
- Flashlights & Batteries.. 99
- Don't Ignore the Leaves.. 99
- Check for Water Leaks... 99

Your Fixed Payment Isn't So Fixed 99
A Closing Note 104

Dedication

I would like to dedicate this book to all of the amazing people that have been there for me throughout life's journey; to my amazing wife, Maiden Gomez, who has always supported me through good and bad times, and whose love has helped me through some of my toughest challenges; to my uncle and aunt, Carlos and Elizabeth Palacios, who provided me with a home when I needed it the most; to my brother Mario Roque whose love and loyalty is unmatched; to Ann Sabbagh, who kindly gave a stranger an opportunity to grow, shine, and succeed.

I dedicate this to all the new friends and family I have made through the mortgage and real estate industries. I have touched the lives of so many people as they have mine. I have been to their weddings, birthday parties, family gatherings, first communions, Christmas Eves, and have even welcomed newborn members of their families into the homes I helped them achieve. I've been warmly welcomed into the homes and lives of so many people with such love. Seeing how many lives I have impacted along the way has made me fall in love with the industry. A home is something so much more than brick and mortar. It's a place where memories are made; we laugh with loved ones, cry through hardships, and feel comfort when we seek escape from the rest of the world. It's the place where we forever hold the fondest and most intimate memories of our lives. I truly feel blessed to be a part of all of these memories.

Lastly, I dedicate this to a good friend whom I have yet to meet but God willing, someday I will, Tony Stark Policci. At one of my lowest points in life, Tony kindly stepped up to help me on a project while I was trying to get back up on my feet. He is a dear friend. He definitely knows how to put my words into perspective.

Introduction

I was tired of seeing people lose unimaginable amounts of money, time, and sanity on failed home purchase transactions. I launched Re-Connect to help people achieve the dream of owning the right home, while also making agents' lives a lot easier. This book isn't about those agents. It's about you the home buyer. I believe everyone can invest and save a lot of money once they understand one basic principle:

> Price Doesn't Matter, Payment Does!

"Price doesn't matter payment does", is a phrase that will change your home buying experience. At its core, it might sound like a riddle to people outside of the industry but I am here to tell you that it absolutely needn't be difficult. This simple guide will tell you everything you need to know. Better yet, it'll do it in a way that you can understand. Let's leave the technical terms to the professionals, and get a grasp of your financial future together. With this book at your side, you'll save a lot of money, and you'll never walk into a transaction blind again.

> **You could say reading this book is a solid investment.**

I am infinitely passionate about helping people make smart financial decisions. Through creative thinking and inventive solutions, everyone can have the investment opportunities they deserve. This book is just one part of the plan to level the playing field of home buying.

Through an extensive 18+ years of real estate, mortgage, underwriting, and loan origination experience with background on both sides of transactions, I've learned a better way than the industry standard of purchasing. This is a book for the buyers; you deserve to get the most bang for your buck, and can only do that by understanding the industry from the inside out.

Most people don't realize there is a direct correlation between mortgage denial and true affordability. "The Consumer Financial Protection Bureau recently released loan-level mortgage lending data submitted by more than 5,600 commercial banks, savings associations, credit unions, and mortgage companies covered by the Home Mortgage Disclosure Act (HMDA)." (Corelogic, 2019). That data showed that 2.65 million loan applications secured by single-family one-to-four-unit properties (including manufactured homes) were *denied*, making the overall denial rate 24.7%. Out of that denial rate, a higher debt-to-income ratio (DTI) was responsible for more than 36.8% of denied home-purchase applications meaning they couldn't even afford the house they were trying to buy. Most of these denials resulted from a flawed system. I have been relentlessly trying to fix this system through the education and software I have designed for the industry (Corelogic, 2019).

About the Author

My name is Julio. I am an entrepreneur, and the inventor of a proprietary system that helps buyers purchase homes based on true affordability. I bring the empathy and human touch that is so imperative within my industry.

I want to help clients avoid disappointment while bringing their real and authentic affordability to the surface. Proving there's no need to "settle" for what you "think" you can afford. Chances are you can do a lot better than you believe.

I have been in the mortgage and real estate industry for more than 18 years and involved in all aspects of the industry. I have taught and educated thousands of first-time home buyers, trained industry professionals, and found tremendous success as a top producing mortgage lender, credit repair specialist, mortgage underwriter, real estate broker-owner, inventor, and entrepreneur.

I am also the founder/owner of Re-Connect, LLC. I am an out-of-the-box thinker and an inventor with patent-pending technology that will change the industry and help buyers shop smarter, not harder. The industry has many flaws, but it has been my life's mission to help people understand it and teach them how to properly purchase a home.

I also know what it's like to start over after hitting rock bottom. I was diagnosed with Crohn's disease at 15 years old, experienced a crippling motorcycle accident at 27, and had major surgery for a stomach tumor at 34.

More than once, I have lost everything, but I have always been able to bounce back. In fact, these experiences have forged in me a heart of gold and a refusal to quit. Now, I am on a new mission. At the age of 44, my goal is to impact the lives of as many people as humanly possible while helping them grow to make wiser, smarter financial decisions.

Chapter 1

True Affordability: How a Mortgage Really Works!

Chapter Introduction

Price Doesn't Matter, Payment Does! Remember those words! To fully grasp what those words mean, you must first understand the home buying process and how a mortgage actually works. You see, the biggest problem in the industry is that buyers generally shop for homes based on educated guesses.

I have spent years perfecting and developing the technology and method to help buyers become more knowledgeable and successful in purchasing their home. I want to make sure the purchase is based on true affordability versus the traditional methods, as most lenders today issue pre-approvals based on educated guesses.

If you reside in the United States. You can always reach out to me, and I will be more than happy to either help or guide you in the right direction. You can visit my website www.juliocroque.com for all of my contact information. With that said, let us jump in!!!

DTI Explained

Let's talk about DTI, Debt to Income. These are percentages used in the mortgage industry to determine if you qualify for a home.

There is a housing ratio and a debt ratio. Both are quite simple and easy to understand. In fact, it is all easy math. The housing ratio is your complete mortgage payment (Principal, Interest, Taxes, Insurance, HOA) divided by your income.

For example, if your entire mortgage payment is $1,800 a month, and your income is $5,000 a month, your housing ratio is 36%.

 Example: $1,800 / $5,000 = 36%

Your total debt ratio is your complete mortgage payment (principal, interest, taxes, insurance, HOA) plus your monthly debt such as car payment, student loans, credit card payments divided by your income.

For example, if your complete mortgage payment is $1,800 a month plus $300 a month in other debt (for a total of $2,100) and your income is $5,000 a month, then your debt ratio is 42%.

 Example: $1,800 + $300 = $2,100 / $5,000 = 42%

So, in this example, your DTI would be 36% / 42%. All loan programs may have different requirements when it comes to DTI.

The Truth Behind a Bank Pre-Approval

Regardless of whether you are buying a $300,000 property or $20,000,000 property, lenders question affordability the same way: can you afford the monthly payment?

Out of the millions of denied mortgages I mentioned in the introduction of this book, a good portion are a result of buyers trying to purchase properties they cannot afford, even though they had a pre-approval letter (a letter which is based on an educated guess).

Now, let's not get ahead of ourselves here. There's a lot more than principal and interest that goes into a mortgage payment, but don't worry! It will all be covered throughout this book.

I was once blown away by a supposed veteran loan officer in the industry. I asked about the pre-approval letter process: the answer that followed absolutely shocked me.

Here is what happened:

After asking how he goes about the pre-approvals, he said he collects documents and sends them to the underwriter. The underwriter then reviews the documents and gives the green light along with a purchase price amount to the loan officer. Thereafter, the loan officer provides the buyer with a pre-approval certificate with a big pre-approval number printed right in the middle of it.

Remember: Price Doesn't Matter, Payment Does

When asked what would happen if the buyer found a property out of the scope of the underwriters' calculations used to determine the payment that gave them that pre-approval amount, he looked at me as if I was speaking a foreign language. As much as I tried to explain it, he was clueless. Then, I asked if he ever has denials, and he answered, "Yes, of course." I asked, "Why?" He replied, "Well, something changed.", and when asked what the changes were, I would simply get the same answers with no further clarification. He was clueless about how this process actually works; leading me to pray for the poor buyers... *may GOD help them*!

If the professionals you rely on have no idea what's going on, how can you as the buyer feel secure?! Remember this story as we continue, and as I explain true affordability.

In short, your pre-approval is all based on a *monthly payment*, **NOT** a purchase price. That payment is determined as a percentage of your monthly income. Since lenders do not know what home you will purchase and the specifics that drive that payment, they base everything on an educated guess.

For example, John Makes $3000 a month. With a conventional loan, he qualifies for a maximum mortgage payment that must include principal, interest, taxes, insurance, private mortgage insurance (PMI), and any applicable HOA (homeowners association) fees. That Payment must be no more than 45% of his income, which is $1350 a month. There are exceptions that go up to 50%

Price Doesn't Matter, Payment Does

depending on the situation, but we will stick with 45% for this example and assume John has no debt.

Now John goes to a bank where the loan officer analyzes this and punches numbers into the system. The loan officer will play around with different scenarios until they come up with what they feel is a reasonable loan amount.

For example:

Purchase Price:	$180,000
Down Payment: 5%	$9,000
Loan Amount:	$171,000
Interest Rate:	4%
Principal and Interest Payment:	$950.00
Monthly Insurance Amount:	$75.00
Monthly Tax Amount:	$300.00
Monthly Private Mortgage Insurance:	$25
TOTAL PAYMENT:	**$1,350.00**

So, now the bank will give John a pre-approval letter for $180,000 based on the above calculation, which is nothing more than an educated guess. It is common practice to do it this way because the bank has absolutely no idea what John will pick for a home. This can cause major problems, though.

If John finds a home where annual taxes **EXCEED** $300 a month (let's say $400 a month), his payment will increase by $100 a month and would essentially disqualify him. He will start the process and potentially spend money on a home he can't even buy because it was out of the scope of what the loan officer calculated. John had no idea because he was relying on the accuracy of the pre-approval letter. Relying on the loan officer's assumptions can result in money being spent on home inspections and appraisals to then only end up with a denial. This problem has caused people to lose millions of dollars nationwide.

Now referring back to my story, you can see why I was shocked that the loan officer was so clueless. Lenders care about *payments, not price*. Two homes with the same price can carry two completely different payments based on other expenses, i.e., taxes, and one can quickly disqualify a person while the other does not.

More for Your Money

Since lenders base their pre-approvals on educated guesses, John could miss out on an even better, more affordable home. He has mistakenly been given the mindset that he only qualifies for $180,000 when in reality he qualifies for a payment, not a price. This has caused millions of home buyers to miss out on opportunities to truly have a better home.

For example:

Purchase Price:	$200,000
Down Payment: 5%	$10,000
Loan Amount:	$190,000
Interest Rate:	4%

Principal and Interest Payment:	$1,045.00
Monthly Insurance Amount:	$75.00
Monthly Tax Amount:	$175.00
Monthly Private Mortgage Insurance:	$29
TOTAL PAYMENT:	**$1,324.00**

You see, in the example above, there was a home for $200,000 that would have carried a lesser payment than the home for $180,000 but the buyer would never, in a million years, have known that. Remember, banks don't care what the price of the home is; they only care whether or not you can afford the monthly payment.

This gets even more mind-boggling when you buy an owner-occupied investment property such as a 2-to 4-family home. If your actual approval is a payment based on a percentage of your income and now you are buying an income-producing property, there is no way to determine the future income of a property you select except by means of an educated guess. This is a recipe for disaster and has caused buyers to miss out on opportunities or end up with a denial due to low rental income, all again due to a flawed system.

Ryan Serhant and I met in New York, and as I was talking to him about my projects, I ran numbers for kicks on some NY properties. I was blown away to see a 4,200 sq ft condo, selling for $13,950,000 carrying the same exact monthly payment as a 9,112 sq ft townhouse listed for $17,500,000 a few blocks away.

That's a 3.5-million-dollar difference for the same payment on a much bigger and nicer property. So, what was the catch?! The condo had a huge common area fee which the townhouse did not, making the payment exactly the same on both. So, if banks lend based on *payment, not price*, you could actually afford either one but your average buyer is unaware of that fact.

Owner Occupied Investment Property

Financing pre-approvals on owner-occupied investment properties can fluctuate tremendously, and can be extremely confusing, so I want to break it all down into its own little segment. Let us take an example with some properties you could find online and see for yourself.

Assume we have a buyer with $3,750 in monthly income interested in two properties. He has the following amount in debt: Car $350; credit cards $118; personal loan $150; student loans $104, for a grand total of $722 a month. Look at how he compares with the following two properties:

10 Merrifield Street

3 Family Building

Rental Income if occupying the first floor:

$2,976, of which the lender will allow you to use 75% $2,232

Total Usable Income for the Purchase:

$5,982 which is $3,750 + $2,232

   Mortgage Payment Info: FHA Loan 3% annual interest rate

Principal & Interest	$1,738.66
Insurance	$170.00
Taxes	$374.75
Mortgage Insurance	$284.35
TOTAL PAYMENT	**$2,567.76**

If you remember the lesson on debt to income you will remember that most loan programs have two ratios. The first is your housing payment divided by your income. The second is your housing payment and monthly liabilities divided by your income. Now on an FHA loan, qualifying ratios are 43% for housing and 55% for housing plus current monthly liabilities.

So, let's do some math:

$2,567.76 divided by total income of $5,982.00 is 42.925% for housing and $2,567.76 plus monthly debt of $722 = $3,289.76 divided by $5,982 = 54.994% for total debt.

Housing: $2,567.76 / $5,982.00 = **42.925%**

Housing + Debt: $2,567.76 + $722 = $3,289.76 / $5,982.00 = **54.994%**

As you can see, it is perfectly qualified with the income.

Now take a look at a different home for this same buyer.

51 Proctor Street

3 Family Building

Rental Income if occupying the first floor:

$1,425 of which the lender will allow you to use 75% $1,068.75

Total Usable Income for the Purchase:

$4,818.75 which is $3,750 + $1,068.75

Mortgage Payment Info: FHA Loan 3% annual interest rate

Principal & Interest	$1,345.39
Insurance	$170.00
Taxes	$408.75
Mortgage Insurance	$220.04
TOTAL PAYMENT	**$2,144.18**

On an FHA loan, qualifying ratios are 43% for housing and 55% for housing plus current monthly liabilities.

So, let's do some math:

$2,144.18 divided by total income of $4,818.75 is 44.497% for housing and $2,144.18 plus monthly debt of $722 = $2,866.18 divided by $4,818.75 = 59.480%.

Housing:	$2,144.18 / $4,818.75 = **44.497%**
Housing + Debt:	$2,144.18 + $722 = $2,866.18 / $4,818.75 = **59.480%**

As you can see, despite the almost $95,000 lesser price tag, this buyer would not be able to afford this property based on the numbers and guidelines.

This has been a huge problem for the buyer as long as I can remember. Some people would then say, "Well, why can't the bank use market rent if the current tenants are paying below-market rent?!" Well, the answer to that is also quite simple. Lenders are not religious and do not lend based on faith. In other words, they are not going to let you borrow money hoping that you will get market rent. They always use safe numbers to ensure that you do not go into foreclosure.

So, to recap, lenders only care about *payment* vs. income, *not price*. There are so many things that drive a mortgage payment that not even two identically priced homes would have the same payment, even if priced the same. The taxes could be different, and the condo fee could be different, the common area fee could be different, the rental income could be different. Save yourself the trouble and be sure to ask a lot of questions!!!!

Chapter 2

Proper Planning

Nothing makes a transaction more successful than proper education and planning. Depending on what your plans and future goals are, you should always have a game plan.

Type of Home

There is a lot that goes into planning for a home. As a first-time homebuyer, you have many options, and depending on what your future plans are, you have to give this a lot of thought and consideration. You see, when you purchase your first property, you can choose anything from a single-family to a four-family home, and depending on the loan program, could put a down payment anywhere from 0% to 5%.

If you have plans of investing in a property, it would be incredibly wise to start with a 2- or 4-family owner-occupied building. Keep in mind you are expected to live in any home you buy as a first-time homebuyer, which is why you get such a good deal with financing. If you purchase a single-family home, for example, and put 3% down with a conventional loan then later decide to purchase a 4-family and want to do it with 0% - 5% down, you won't be able to do so. You now own a single-family home, and the lender will see that 4-family as a pure investment requiring you to put down around 25% and pay a much higher rate for it being an investment property. Low down payments and low-interest rates are for owner-occupied properties only, and now that you own a single-family, the lender will find it hard to believe that you will rent out the home you reside in to move in with tenants.

Now, let us look at a different possible scenario where you decide to purchase a multi-family home first, i.e. a 3-family owner-occupied property. You could purchase this property with very little money down because it is your first home. Many programs require anywhere from 0% down to 5% down, so let's assume you purchased this building with an FHA loan at 3.5% down.

You are required to live in the property for one year. After that, you are free to purchase another home. You could then purchase a single-family home with conventional financing after putting 5% down and become the owner of a piece of investment property along with the single-family home you wanted so much. This is possible because a lender could understand you wanting to leave the multi-family and wanting to get away from your tenants to live in the privacy of a single-family.

Let us take this a step further. You can also own more than one multi-family with little money down (I have accomplished it many times). Say you purchase a multi-family home, such as a 3-family with two bedrooms per unit, with an owner-occupied conventional community lending product with 0% or 5% down, depending on the loan program. Later, your situation changes, and two bedrooms are no longer accommodating the family. You could then purchase another 3- or 4-family owner-occupied building that suits the needs of your family with an FHA loan putting 3.5% for a down payment.

Situations such as this are very possible as long as you have a very good reason for the purchase. You still have to live in the new property. Otherwise, it would be considered mortgage fraud, which is a huge NO - NO, and you have to have very strong reasons behind your purchase in order for the lender to accept such a transaction. Reasons that could make such a situation possible would be needing more space, such as extra bedrooms or bathrooms, needing to be closer to work (and not just by 5 minutes closer), and needing parking space (assuming your current home has no off-street parking).

You are only required to live in the second property for a year if using FHA, and then after that, you can purchase your single-family home at only 5% down with a conventional loan. In a nutshell, with a strategy like this, you could own three properties and have a really nice portfolio, which is a great addition to your retirement nest.

In some rare situations, you can even own up to three owner-occupied buildings if you are a US veteran and have a VA loan available. I have done this a small handful of times. Again, you must have strong reasons behind your purchase as the lender will question the heck out of it, but it's not impossible! In a situation like this, you would use a conventional loan first such as a community lending product like MassHousing, then FHA or VA, and for the third, FHA or VA depending on which one you used for the second purchase. This is INSANE! You could buy a 3-to-4 family owner-occupied investment property with 0% to 5% down. That 0% to 5% down is *only* with a conventional community lending option as traditional conventional options do not offer 0% to 5% down. Then, you could purchase another property with the VA with 0% down, then another with FHA with 3.5% down. Investors will hate you! This is such a huge advantage in building a beautiful real estate retirement portfolio. Then, you can move on to your last single-family purchase with 5% down. It's crazy, right-yet possible.

Budgeting

Proper budgeting is crucial. Even if a lender says that you qualify for a certain amount, you still have to do your own due diligence in budgeting for what you can truly afford. A lender may think your maximum housing payment is $1,800 a month based on what they see for expenses on your credit report, but what a lender does not see are your day-to-day spending habits that do not report on your credit.

Some of these expenses could be as simple as gas, your daily Starbucks fix, or your routine dinner and a movie every weekend with the family. These expenses add up, and no matter how good of a lender you have, they have no way of knowing that your affordability is more like $1,500 a month and not the $1,800 the computer calculates. Take a little bit of time to analyze your spending habits, and calculate what you truly feel you can afford.

A good safety net for buying a home is to add 10% in additional costs to the monthly payment. This will help cover things like maintenance and upkeep. The reason for this is because many people forget there is no longer a landlord to call if something breaks or if things need updating. You are it. It's your house now, and it is all *your* responsibility. Try to save those additional funds before buying the home to see if there are any impacts on your lifestyle. You may be surprised to see that some adjustments will need to be made, such as no more Starbucks!

Once you purchase your first multifamily building, here is another small but super important tip when budgeting for a 2- to 4- family owner-occupied investment property. You should still pay rent! Even if you find a property with enough rental income to cover all or most of your mortgage, don't make the mistake of thinking you can live rent-free. That is the first step to failure. Still pay to yourself what you formerly would have in rent!

These are income producing properties, and the unit you live in plays a huge role in their success. Why? Well, these properties require maintenance and may sometimes have tenant issues that require extra funds. By paying rent and saving that money, you will be prepared for any potential rainy days ahead. A key part of successful financial growth is financial discipline, so instead of thinking you're rent-free and using that money to vacation or buy a new car, save it and prepare for your future growth. Those vacations and cars can come later.

Credit

Proper planning also involves an understanding of your credit. Credit is so misunderstood. Some people think that building strong credit means getting into a ton of debt, which is very wrong. You would be surprised to learn that many people think if you have a credit card with a $2,000 limit, all $2,000 needs to be spent in order to build good credit; nothing could be further from the truth. The purpose of your having a credit card is to show fiscal responsibility. Your ability to consistently utilize the available credit is being monitored and reported. Using only a small fraction of that limit is ideal, and creates a history of how much control you have over your spending. Anyone can spend money, which is the easy part. Not everyone knows how to control themselves, and that's what the credit bureaus are monitoring. They are analyzing your self-control.

Two of the biggest impacts on credit are late payments and high credit card balances. These are huge! You need to pay your bills on time, and you need to keep your credit card balances low. Low credit card balances can tremendously impact your credit. Traditionally, people are taught to keep a 30% balance, I have seen over 10,000 credit reports, and the biggest increase I see in credit scores when it comes to credit card balances is when you have a 10% balance or less. Also, important to note is that paying the card down to absolute zero can give you a slightly lower score than if you just keep a small balance on the card.

I have seen credit scores increase by over 100 points within 30 days by simply paying down some balances. Small credit cards are sometimes the easiest fix to your credit. If you have a small credit card with a $500 limit and owe $450 on it, you could see a huge increase to your credit score with a simple $400 payment. You see, it is all based on percentages. It is so easy to max out your credit card when you have a small credit card limit, vs. a credit card with a $10,000 limit. So, it is highly suggested to pay down your credit card balances as much as possible at least 45 days before applying for a mortgage loan to maximize your score as much as possible.

Another issue with credit most people don't realize is how important it is to *have* a credit card. Unfortunately, revolving credit (your credit cards) account for 30 % of your credit score. So, if you do not have a credit card, you are missing out on that significant percentage. Now, I have come across a lot of people who start to panic as soon as I tell them they need a credit card to increase their score, but as soon as I explain the reasons behind that statement, they begin to understand. Your credit won't go anywhere without the conservative use of a credit card. Remember, this is all about financial responsibility and control, so don't go nuts and max out your card all at once. It is not a contest to see who can spend the most money.

Building credit with a credit card can be as simple as paying a recurring bill with it. Do you like Netflix? Set it on auto pay and pay with your credit card. It really is that simple, and by giving the card frequent usage, you will drastically improve your score.

Another factor people fail to consider is having too many credit cards, and then having some of them close out on you. A key part of your credit score is based on your account history. When you fail to use a credit card, the creditor could decide to close that account, causing a decrease in your score. Why would this cause a decrease? It's because you lose the account history on that card. So, when applying for a home, make sure to keep all your cards active and keep a minimal balance on them to maximize your credit score.

Co-Signing

This is important: beware of co-signing for anyone! Co-signing can have tremendous adverse effects on your ability to buy a home. If the person you co-sign for doesn't stay on top of the payments, you will be held equally responsible. Also, it's important to remember that if you say yes, you will be adding more debt to your current scenario, thereby increasing your debt-to-income ratio.

The only way to possibly get the lender to exclude that debt would be to prove that the person has made twelve payments from a bank account non-affiliated with your name. Another co-signing death wish many people do, is putting their name on another person's student loans. Even if those payments are deferred, the lender will take 1% of the balance and add it to your liabilities as a monthly payment. So, if you co-sign a $20,000 student loan balance, and it's deferred, the lender will still add a $200 per month payment to your monthly liabilities.

To summarize, here is a quick rundown on the most important things to keep an eye out for when it comes to credit.

- Keep low credit card balances and pay them down 45 days before applying for a mortgage if necessary. Even if you think you have excellent credit at 740, and are offered the best rate, you can still decrease your private mortgage insurance if your credit jumps a little higher to a 760 or 780.
- Do not apply for anything unless it's an absolute emergency, and do not close accounts as this can decrease your score. The only exception to this is if you don't have a credit card. If you don't have one, open one up, even if it is a secure credit card.
- Pay your bills on time. This is huge as I have seen a single late payment decrease scores by as much as 40 to 60 points
- Don't co-sign for anyone. No further explanation is needed.
- Make sure any past bills or payments aren't in hiding, such as medical copayments, cell phone bills, or final utility payments. You can't afford to have them sneak up on you without warning during the home buying process.
- Last and most importantly, ***do not*** add new debt of any kind.

All of these things can drastically decrease your score so pay close attention to them before you actually apply for a home loan.

Required Funds

Before going into the required funds that you need to purchase a home, it's essential to keep in mind that you cannot borrow funds for this transaction. For example, asking for money from a friend, borrowing against a credit card, or taking out a personal bank loan is not allowed. The funds that are allowed for the purchase can be any of the following: your own funds, gift funds from friends or family, and funds from a 401k or retirement account. Borrowing funds from a 401k or retirement account is considered OK because it is your money, and you are borrowing from yourself. You can also use money from a home equity loan. Money from grants is also allowed.

The amount you need to purchase a home is really going to depend on the type of home and the type of financing you will be applying for. I will go over this in more detail when we discuss loan programs, but here is a general idea and example:

> If you are buying a $200,000 single-family home with an FHA program and your down payment is 3.5%, you will need $7,000 for a down payment.

Aside from that, you will also need money for closing costs and inspections which amount to roughly another 3% or $6,000, for an estimated total of $13,000. Now, the closing costs can, of course, be negotiated with the seller, and you can request to have them pay for it, but in a competitive sellers' market, the more you ask for, the less your chances are of getting the home.

If you were buying a multi-family such as a 3-family, you would also need reserves. When a lender says you need reserves, they refer to several months' worth of your mortgage payment (the amount depends on the loan program) being placed in some sort of a savings account or 401k. For FHA, there are three months of reserves required when buying a 3- to 4-family home. Let's refer back to my example above. If the mortgage payment on a $200,000 3-family home is $1,500 a month, you would need to add an additional $4,500 in reserves added to your budget, for a total of $17,500. Again, a seller may help you with some of these costs if you are able to negotiate it into the deal.

It is very important to avoid cash deposits during this process. When I say cash, I mean walking up to your bank teller and giving him/her a stack of Benjamin Franklins. Cash is prohibited in the purchase of a home. All funds for the purchase of a home must be verified, and unfortunately, that cannot be done with cash.

Here is an example of a common mistake people make when it comes to their money:

> After getting a huge tax refund (let's say $10,000), some people don't want their money in the bank, so they decide to withdraw those funds. Four months later, when they are ready to buy a home, they try to redeposit the $10,000, but guess what?! They aren't allowed to use those funds because it is impossible to prove that it's the same $10,000 withdrawn all those months ago.

Banks will review the last two to three months of bank statements, so if they spot cash activity, they will question it, and 99.9999% of the time will not allow you to use it. One of the very few circumstances where cash is acceptable is if, within the same day, you withdraw cash from one bank account and immediately deposit the exact same amount into another account. They will be considered acceptable if the amounts are a match and occur on the same day.

Now, this does not mean that all cash deposits are prohibited as there is some amount of flexibility, albeit very small. Finance guidelines state that any cash deposit over 1% of your loan amount is considered a large deposit and must be verified. I always tell my buyers as good practice, and to be safe, that any large deposit would be the lesser of the following two: 1% of the loan amount or 25% of your monthly income. For example, if you are buying a home that is $200,000 and getting a loan for $190,000, then 1% of that is $1,900 but if your income to qualify is $4,000 a month, and 25% of that is $1,000, then avoid deposits of over $1,000 in cash to reduce the risk of not being able to use the funds. Use the lesser of the two, and you will always be safe. Keep in mind that a lender will look out for and add multiple deposits within a certain amount of time. So, if you make a bunch of small cash deposits on the same day that adds up to a large amount, they could consider it as one deposit and will not let you use the funds for closing.

You must plan ahead, and if you have cash, get that money in the bank a few months before starting the home buying process. It is not uncommon to see people save money at home but to avoid any issues with financing, you have to get all your cash in the bank as soon as possible.

Getting gift money is an acceptable source of funds as well, but those funds must also be verified. Gift funds should be in the form of a check or bank transfer to properly document the source of the funds.

The lender will require that the person gifting you the funds provide a bank statement to show they had that money available. Like you, any cash deposits into their accounts will also get questioned and possibly rejected. It is essential to make sure they already had the funds available and in their account.

Other acceptable sources of funds other than your own money and gift funds could come from a 401k, stocks, or other accessible types of savings or retirement accounts.

It is also important that once you have decided on the type of home and program you are going to go with, that you start saving the required funds if you don't already have the money available.

Chapter 3

Understanding Income

Your understanding and calculations of income may not be the same as the lenders, so you should understand how income is calculated. In this chapter, we will take a good look at several of the most common types of income.

W2 Income

A W2 employee is someone who works for someone else and receives income with taxes taken out. If you are a salaried W2 employee, your income will be much easier to figure out than an hourly employee's income because an hourly employee's income can vary, whereas a salaried employees' pay is usually consistent over long stretches of time. When a lender calculates income, it is not always as easy as just calculating hours worked by an hourly rate. Lenders also look at your year-to-date income to make sure you are earning a consistent and steady income. You better believe they will question any inconsistencies!

For example, if you work 40 hours a week at $20 an hour ($800 a week, $41,600 per year) and apply for a mortgage mid-year, your paystubs should reflect $20,800. Rather, if they show $17,200 due to unpaid time off, or shortened days for appointments, expect to be questioned, and your qualifying income may even get reduced.

Regardless of the reasons why the income is reflected at a lower number, a lender may not feel comfortable giving you credit because, in their eyes, that income does not exist. So, when planning on purchasing a home, it is important to make sure you have consistent, steady, and equal paychecks.

Using Multiple Jobs

Nowadays, it is common to see people hold more than one job. Lenders are okay with allowing you to use multiple income sources, but as with any other income, they are looking for consistency.

Sometimes, if one job is not enough to qualify for a home, many people mistakenly think they can simply pick up any random job, and the lender will accept both incomes. This is definitely not the case. A good rule of thumb to use is to hold your jobs for at least two years. There are cases with exceptions using one year, but to be safe, two years is the key.

If you are able to steadily and consistently hold two jobs, a lender will have no problem letting you use both jobs to qualify for a home. In the case you have two jobs but insufficient time with both, the lender will only allow the use of one of the two jobs, not both.

Commissioned and Variable Income

From car sales associates to loan officers, there is a huge variety of commissioned employees out there. The use of commission income is entirely acceptable, and again, the rule of thumb is two years. Lenders look for two years of steady commission income and will do a two-year average with those numbers. If the most recent year is lower than the previous, they will use the lower of the two as lenders always use safe numbers.

Using one year of commission income is possible, but only on a case-by-case basis, and will be based on compensating factors. Such factors could be, but are not limited to, great credit, substantial reserves, significant down payment, strong previous work history, and so on.

Variable incomes a lender may consider acceptable are incomes such as bonuses, tips, and overtime, all of which must be steady and dependable. Only with a good history may these incomes be used. For instance, if you have a solid 40-hour per week job and suddenly started working overtime without having a history of ever doing so, you would not be allowed to use the income. You would have to have two years of consistently working overtime.

Let's move on to a different type of variable income such as drivers, who get paid by mileage, stops, or loads. This also requires a two-year history. As this income is inconsistent and can vary, a lender will want to see the average. It is still possible if you have less than two years that the income can be used on a case-by-case basis, but most likely, the lender will average it out with whatever other income you had prior to that job.

Since there are too many different types of variable incomes to go over, the easy thing to do is just to remember the basic rule of thumb: two years is generally the required amount of time for employment history, but anything less than two years can be used with compensating factors.

Self-Employed Borrowers

Self-employment is a big topic, and I could write another book just on that alone, but here is the gist of how it relates to buying a home. To start, self-employed borrowers need two years of self-employment. From there, the lender will look at your net after expenses, not gross.

They will do a two-year average of your net income, and if the most recent year is lower, they will use the most recent year only, but you still need two years of self-employment.

If your most recent year of self-employment is more than 20% lower in net income than the prior year, the lender may reject the income in its entirety (unless you have a very strong reason for the decrease). So, let's see how this would work with the following example:

> Let's say you have a construction business, and in 2018 you grossed $800,000 with a net of $50,000, and in 2019 you grossed $900,000 with a net of $75,000. The lender will add 2018 and 2019 net incomes, with a total of $125,000, and divide that total by 24 for a monthly income of $5,208 per month.

Many people do not know that Freddie Mac has different rules for self-employed borrowers. They allow you to use the most recent year of tax returns instead of two years, giving you a better advantage due to a higher average.

In the previous example, the self-employed borrower would have been able to use $75,000 in income divided by 12, which is $6,250 per month instead of $5,208 per month, making a huge difference in his qualifications, but there's a catch. The borrower must prove five years in business by means of licenses or a CPA letter. This method would not work for a newly established business.

Here are a few tips for self-employed borrowers:

Not all of your expenses are a total loss. You could have extra income you didn't even know about which is partially dependent upon which loan product you choose.

Let's take a look at a possible scenario that could be huge in helping you qualify for a home:

Example 2018 Schedule C

Line 7 Gross Income:	$120,000
Expenses	
Line 8 Advertising	$6,000
Line 9 Car and Truck Expenses	$12,000
Line 11 Contract Labor	$25,000
Line 12 Depletion	$2,000
Line 13 Depreciation	$13,000
Line 15 Insurance	$2,000
Line 18 Office Expenses	$6,000

Line 22 Supplies	$3,000
Line 30 Business Use of Home	$11,000
Total Expenses	$80,000
Net Income	**$40,000**

Example 2019 Schedule C

Line 7 Gross Income:	$150,000

Expenses

Line 8 Advertising	$8,000
Line 9 Car and Truck Expenses	$18,000
Line 11 Contract Labor	$30,000
Line 12 Depletion	$2,000
Line 13 Depreciation	$13,000
Line 15 Insurance	$3,000
Line 18 Office Expenses	$8,000
Line 22 Supplies	$6,000
Line 30 Business Use of Home	$11,000
Total Expenses	$99,000
Net Income	**$51,000**

In this scenario, you would think you have an income of $40,000 + $51,000, and when divided by 24, it would end at $3,791.67 per month. What a lot of people don't realize is that with most loan programs, there are expenses you can add back into your income such as mileage (line 9), depletion (line 12), depreciation (line 13), or business use of home (line 30). In this scenario, that is $82,000 in expenses, which can now be counted as income. Wow! Think of how powerful that is.

You paid taxes on an income of $91,000 between both years, but the bank is giving you back $82,000 worth of expenses to increase your income to $91,000 + $82,000 equaling $173,000, which, when divided by 24, is $7,208.33 per month instead of $3,791.67. This is huge, as your qualifying income literally almost doubled.

The above scenario is critical to understand, so be sure to consult with your CPA. You could potentially have more income than you thought for the purchase of your home. Keep this in mind if you operate an in-home child daycare (see line 30, 'business use of the home' on schedule C of your tax forms) or if you drive for a company like Uber (that's line 9, 'mileage deduction' on schedule C). Both of these could offer huge benefits for you!

*Day Care Providers, don't miss out on these tax breaks. https://www.irs.gov/publications/p587

Schedule E Rental Income

Owning rental property is a fantastic way to build net worth. When you start to own property it's essential to understand how Schedule E works. Lenders do not look at your gross rental income.

It does not matter how much money your 3-unit building makes because if you're claiming all sorts of expenses, your income could be $0 or even negative!

Lenders look at Line number 21 for the specific property to see if there is income or loss. Just like on a Schedule C, there are certain line items that get added back to the income. Here is what they allow.

Line 9 -	Insurance
Line 12 -	Mortgage Interest
Line 16 -	Taxes
Line 18 -	Depreciation

If your income on line 21 is negative, by adding back those other lines you could end up with a positive income. Depending on your situation, a lender may use the most recent tax return to evaluate the income or, in some cases, may compute a two-year average. You must check with your lender to see what your situation will be.

If you purchased income-producing property less than a year ago, and still have not filed tax returns to show the income, you will need to show leases, and the total usable income will be 75% of the gross income. As an example, if your rental income is $1,000, then the lender will only use $750 of that income for qualifying purposes.

Suppose you plan on buying another home and renting out your current apartment or house with certain loan programs. In that case, you can use that departure property rental income as long as you have a signed lease and a copy of the deposit check to lease the premises.

This income is usually allowed on conventional loans and not FHA loans unless you move 100 miles away or more from your current residence. You will also only be allowed to use 75% of that income. After you know the usable net rental income, it is subtracted from the complete mortgage payment of principal, interest, taxes, HOA, and insurance to determine if you have positive or negative rental income that can be used.

Social Security, Retirement, Child Support, and Foster Care Income

There are other types of income that can be used too, such as social security, retirement, child support, or foster care income. If you have retirement social security income, you can use it to qualify for a home, and the nontaxable portion (which will show on your tax returns) can be grossed up by 15%.

For example, if you have $1,000 per month in nontaxable retirement social security income, you can gross it up by 15% to $1,150 per month.

Suppose you have other types of social security income, such as social security disability or social security for your children. In that case, you must prove a minimum continuance of three years to use that income.

So, if you get social security income for a 16-year-old child that stops at age 18, then you would not be able to use that income.

Unlike a second job, you do not need to have been receiving the income for two years in order to use it, as long as the income is permanent or proof of a three-year continuance has been provided. If you have any type of retirement income, such as a pension, you can also use this and combine it with your social security income.

Child support income can also be used, but only if the income will continue for three years and can be supported with solid documentation. You will need proof of receipt for the income for the past three to six months, as well as a divorce decree or court documents showing the approved child support amount. If your child support income is simply a verbal agreement and no further documentation can be provided to support the payments received, then you will not be able to use it.

Foster care income can also be used. Most foster care income is given in the form of a stipend and is nontaxable, and therefore not reported on your tax returns. The lender will need a two-year payment history from the foster care provider to determine the usable amount, along with a letter explaining your daily stipend and recent proof of payments. You can also use this income in conjunction with other income as long as you have a two-year history with both. This income can also be grossed up just like the social security income if it is nontaxable.

Chapter 4

Loan Programs

It is impossible to go over every single loan program out there. In this chapter, I plan on covering the most common programs used by lenders today. As a side note, that whole thing you hear about needing 20% down is just a myth.

Even if you already own a home and are simply upgrading to something better, or if you owned a home in the past, that still does not mean you need 20% down. You usually see these types of larger down payment requirements on jumbo loans, not on standard conventional loans.

I know that quite a few people tend to balk at the mention of taking out a loan, as well. Honestly? Don't! I had to take one out when I first purchased a house, and so do a lot of people. Trying to come up with the amount of money it would take to purchase a house without qualifying for a loan of some sort is a fool's errand. You will end up working yourself straight into the grave and never getting any closer to holding your own set of keys.

This list should give you a little bit of an idea about which places are going to be the most feasible for you to apply to.

Each lending program has its own process of determination and elimination, so make sure to carefully read up on each one of them. Don't be afraid to try and apply to more than one of these lending programs.

Keep in mind that guidelines in lending programs are always changing, and the following information could be outdated. So always ask a lot of questions when applying for your mortgage.

Overlays

This is extremely important to understand before getting into some of the different types of loan programs that exist. Some of these loan programs are government programs, such as FHA, VA, and USDA, while others are Fannie and Freddie Mac products. What generally happens is that these government, Fannie, or Freddie products are issued a set of guidelines or rules, and are then made available to lenders. These lenders now have the option to create additional guidelines and restrictions to add to the ones already created by HUD, Fannie, or Freddie since they are lending their money. This can make financing even more difficult for some people, and you may even see a bank require 20% down instead of the normal 5%, simply because the lender wants to add additional requirements.

A good example is FHA, Federal Housing Administration, which will lend down to a 580-credit score with as little as 3.5% down, but since a lot of lenders find that to be far too risky, they will add additional overlays. For example, they may refuse to lend to a 580-credit score and change their minimum to a 640.

This is important to know because you should always ask to see if the lender you plan on working with has overlays. If they do, learn how their additional guidelines could affect you. If the lender has no overlays, then you'll have a much smoother transaction. They will usually be easier to work with because they simply go off of HUD, Fannie, or Freddie guidelines without adding any additional terms.

FHA

An FHA insured loan is a mortgage insurance backed mortgage loan provided by the US Federal Housing Administration. It's a form of federal assistance that has historically allowed those with a lower income to still purchase a home. It's aimed toward new house owners and not real estate investors. Due to this, the house must be owner-occupied for at least a year.

FHA is an extremely popular loan program. A lot of people think it is just a first-time homebuyer program, but in fact it can be used by anyone and has no income restrictions. One of the upsides of FHA is they are a bit more lenient with credit and rates than conventional financing. So, people with a lower credit score can get better terms of financing with FHA vs. conventional. FHA will lend to people with scores in the 500's, which is almost unheard of with any other loan program out there.

Also, for people that had a previous foreclosure, they are able to purchase a home three years after foreclosure vs. the seven-year wait requirement of conventional financing. For those with a bankruptcy, they can purchase a home two years after discharge vs. the four-year wait requirement of conventional financing and for those with a chapter 13, they can even buy while in chapter 13 with trustee approval.

These leniencies allow people to get into homeownership a lot quicker during life's serious challenges. FHA also allows the purchase of any type of home from a single-family to a 4-family owner-occupied investment property with as little as 3.5% down. You are only allowed to have one FHA loan at a given time, and cannot have multiple unless you have strong reasons such as moving out of state for employment.

Some of FHA's drawbacks are the government funding fee, which is 1.75% of the loan. This usually gets financed. Also, unless you are putting 10% down, the monthly MI (mortgage insurance) on an FHA loan is permanent on a 30 year mortgage. FHA is also fairly strict with property conditions where conventional financing is much more lenient. There is a lot that goes into all of this, and that is why the importance of working with the right team of knowledgeable professionals is paramount.

FHA also has a lot more flexibility as to how much you can borrow. Their ratios can go as high as 43% for housing and 55% for total debt, which will give you more flexibility if you have one too many credit cards or a high car payment. I have seen these ratios hit as high as 46.99% for housing and 56.99% for total debt. Most other financing products limit you at 45% or 50%, with some even lower. So, FHA is a good option if your situation warrants it.

Conventional

Traditionally when we hear about conventional financing, we think of Fannie Mae and Freddie Mac. Both are incredibly similar, and both are highly driven by credit scores and down payment, which means the better the credit score you have, the better the PMI and rate will be. For owner-occupied properties, both require a minimum of 5% down; for an owner-occupied two-family investment property, both require a minimum of 15% down, but for an owner-occupied 3- or 4-family investment property, they differ slightly. Fannie Mae requires a minimum down payment of 25%, and Freddie Mac requires a minimum down payment of 20%.

For investment properties, they are both the same, whereas a single-family investment property will require 15% down, and a 2- or 4-family investment property will require a 25% minimum down payment.

Recently, conventional loans have started to require that you provide 12 months proof of rent to use rental income to qualify. In other words, if you are buying a 3-family owner-occupied income property and need the rental income from the other two units to qualify, you must prove that you paid your current rent on time for the past 12 months. This can be done with canceled rent checks or a letter from the building's management company.

Lenders will not accept letters from private landlords for this. So, if you pay rent in cash to a private landlord, it can be a problem and difficult to prove. Lenders will not accept the receipts that you can easily pick up at Staples as proof, either. Some cash apps may be acceptable since you can see the same consistent withdrawal from your personal bank account to the cash app every month. Just keep in mind that if you need to use rental income to qualify, you must have solid proof of rent.

With regular conventional loans, the maximum DTI is 45% with certain case-by-case scenarios reaching as high as 50%. Unlike FHA that has two ratios which are 43% for housing and 55% for total debt, conventional just looks at one overall. Basically, it is looking at how much house and debt you can afford.

Conventional financing is also strict on credit, requiring a minimum score of 620 plus seven years out of foreclosure and four years out of bankruptcy. Keep in mind that since conventional financing is highly driven by credit score, trying to apply for a conventional loan with a 620 score will not give you favorable terms. You would most likely be better off with FHA if you have a score that low versus a conventional loan.

Fannie Mae HomeReady

HomeReady is designed to help first-time home buyers. The minimum required down payment for a single-family purchase is 3%, which is great. HomeReady also offers more leniencies with rates and lower PMI but there is always a catch, isn't there?! Of course, there is. HomeReady does have income restrictions, so you have to check to see what the income restrictions are for the area you live in. HomeReady is also mostly used for single-family or condo purchases, as they really do not have any special perks for owner-occupied investment properties.

*HomeReady income lookup tool:
https://ami-lookup-tool.fanniemae.com/amilookuptool/

Freddie Mac HomePossible

HomePossible shares all of HomeReady's great features but also includes an extra incentive which allows you to purchase a 3- to 4- family owner-occupied investment property with only 15% for a down payment instead of the industry standard of 20% to 25%. This is such a huge plus!

Of course, they have income restrictions just like HomeReady yet this gives an incredible opportunity to those who may need to buy another 2- to 4- family, owner-occupied property in the future. You never know what the future may bring, so if you are able to use HomePossible to purchase an owner-occupied investment property, then you still have the opportunity to purchase another 2- to 4- family owner-occupied investment property using FHA with as little as 3.5% for a down payment. If you use an FHA loan first to purchase a 2- to 4- family owner-occupied property, then try to use HomePossible. It may not work out because of the income restrictions HomePossible has as you would have the income from two multi-family properties, plus your own income, which may disqualify you, but if you can use it, HomePossible is definitely the way to go.

*HomePossible income lookup tool:
https://sf.freddiemac.com/working-with-us/affordable-lending/home-possible-eligibility-map

VA

VA loans are the best! If you are a US Veteran and have a VA loan available, don't miss out on all of the perks it can offer. You can purchase any owner-occupied property from 1 – 4 residential units with 0% down and no monthly mortgage insurance. Not only is that crazy, but it is the chance of a lifetime! Although VA loans share many of FHA's credit leniencies and property restrictions, they are still a great option.

With the VA loan, you will be charged a one-time funding fee, just like FHA. The amount of this fee will vary, depending on the branch you served, but it can be financed. So, to any US vets out there, don't miss out on such a great loan. The DTI on a VA loan is lower than an FHA loan at 41%, but not having the monthly MI can give you a lower, more comfortable payment, making this an awesome loan to have. Strategizing and using this loan to start an investment portfolio is an incredible advantage that others would die for. Can you imagine buying an owner-occupied investment property using a conventional community product, then a second property using an FHA loan, then a third one using a VA loan?! That's insane, yet very possible.

USDA

A USDA loan is granted by the US Department of Agriculture and is meant for the Rural Development program. It's directed towards small communities, so you cannot use a USDA loan in larger cities or towns.

USDA loans offer a great 100% financing option for single-family homes and other select properties in rural areas.

USDA also offers very low monthly mortgage insurance and a low onetime funding fee of 1%. There are income restrictions to a USDA loan, but they are fairly reasonable.

The one thing a lot of loan officers tend to overlook on a USDA loan, is that the income restrictions are based on the whole entire household and not just the individual borrower applying. Yes, that's right, even people who are not on the loan but live with you and have income, must be declared and that income will be applied towards the income restrictions. Also, another drawback to a USDA loan is that the DTI is lower than most other products at 29% for housing and 41% for total debt.

Finally, these loans can take longer than your average loan because your file must be sent to USDA for review before closing which can make the process much longer.

*USDA income lookup tool: https://eligibility.sc.egov.usda.gov/eligibility/incomeEligibilityAction.do

Community Grant Programs

With just a little bit of homework, you can find some community grant programs to apply for too. These programs usually work in conjunction with some of the previously mentioned loan programs, such as FHA and some of the Fannie or Freddie products. Combining the two is what allows for 100% financing. If you are in the state of Massachusetts, MassHousing has a good program, and in the state of Rhode Island, there is Rhode Island Housing.

Connecticut has Connecticut Housing Finance Authority, Florida has Florida Housing, Texas has Texas State Affordable Housing – this is just a sampling of what is out there, and all are absolutely worth looking into. There are also city programs that give you cash back you can use with any program as long as you qualify. For example, the city of Worcester, MA, has a $5,000 down payment assistance program, and the city of Springfield, MA, has a $2,500 down payment assistance program.

Programs like these can be used to buy owner-occupied, multi-family properties from 1-4 units with 0% to 5% for a down payment! How awesome is that?

Are you living in a different state? Don't worry! There are other great programs as well, but you have to find participating lenders. Chenoa Fund has great 100% financing options as well as Land Home Financial Services, Inc., but they use brokers and established lenders with these programs.

One of the most common mistakes people make when looking at these 100% finance options is thinking they don't need any money to purchase the home, which simply is not true. Just because you are getting the down payment doesn't mean you won't have closing costs, that you won't have to put a deposit down to get the house off the market, or that you won't have to pay for inspections or insurance.

Even with 100% financing, you still need some cash for other expenses. Remember that closing costs can be negotiated with the seller as a seller credit (also known as a seller concession), but in a competitive market, the more you ask for, the least likely a seller will accept your offer. So be prepared.

Chapter 5

Getting a Pre-Approval

Unless you are going to come up with the entire cost of the house in one go and pay it fully out of pocket – which is unlikely for anyone not currently having their name listed on the end credits of a blockbuster hit – you are going to need to figure out how much a lender is willing to lend you.

The Secret to a Smooth Transaction

First, you need a good team that can work well together (we will go over that in the next chapter).

Second, you need to be super organized. Sloppy paperwork and lack of attention to detail can cause delays and issues during the home buying process.

Third, you need an amazing loan officer.

One of the biggest problems within the industry is that just because you have a pre-approval letter that approval is guaranteed. Well, guess what?! A pre-approval is actually pretty useless. A loan officer can screw it up royally, and you could end up losing money. The kicker here is that there is absolutely nothing you can do about it. So, choose carefully and make sure you work with someone well-versed and experienced. Their lack of product and guideline knowledge could adversely affect you.

Lastly, keep in mind that lenders traditionally base their work on educated guesses, as unfortunate as that is. There is no way for a lender to know what type of property you will be buying in the future. It is highly recommended that you ask questions before proceeding with a home offer, especially if it's an income-producing owner-occupied, multi-family home.

If you reside in the United States. You can always reach out to me, and I will be more than happy to either help or guide you in the right direction. You can visit my website www.juliocroque.com for all of my contact information. With that said, let us jump in!!!

Organization is the Key

Here is a list of 10 common items usually needed to get a pre-approval. Depending on your specific situation, other documents may be required. Remember, organization is the key.

1. **W2s and Tax Returns:** All you need are the **last two years** of federal 1040 returns and all schedules. You do not need to provide any state returns. If you have a Schedule C for self-employment, a Schedule E for other properties owned, or Corporate K-1s, make sure you include them. Simply take a good look at your tax returns, and you will see what is needed. The front page of your taxes alone is not acceptable.

2. **Bank statements:** This is to show you have enough funds to close. Be sure to include all pages and make sure you bring actual statements from the **most recent two months**. Most banks allow you to print online monthly statements, but if the printouts do not have your name, bank info, or account number, they won't be accepted. If there is no current month available, you should bring a transaction summary accompanied by two months of complete bank statements. The printout of your balance alone is not acceptable as lenders need to see all transactions of money coming in and out of your accounts.

3. **Pay stubs:** Be ready to provide **two of your most recent pay stubs** and make sure they have all year-to-date earnings as well as your name. Remember, a lender will look at your year-to-date earnings to make sure you pace the income you claim to make.
If you were affected by Covid-19 and took some time off work, were furloughed, or your employer laid you off for a couple of months due to the situation, that is fine. You just need to let the lender know ahead of time to make sure they take the steps to calculate the income properly.

4. **Identification:** Make sure you have current unexpired IDs, such as a driver's license or passport. If you also have your social security card handy, include that as well.

5. **Additional properties:** If you own other properties, you will need the most recent mortgage statements, insurance declaration pages, and tax bills. If you have tenants and have rental income, the leases will be needed to support claimed rental income. Banks look at rental income in a very similar way to self-employment, so be careful with your losses.

6. **Corporations:** If you own an S Corp or any other type of corporation or partnership, and file separate corporate taxes, be sure to bring the last two years of those tax returns, as well as any K-1s or W2s your company may have issued to you.

7. **Investments:** If you have any retirement or investment accounts, such as a 401k, ROTH IRA, stocks, or bonds, make sure to also bring their complete statements. Usually, these types of statements are quarterly statements. Even if these funds are not being used, it strengthens your file and can be used as reserves if needed. Although you do not need to touch or withdraw those funds if using as reserves, a lender may ask you for terms and conditions of withdrawal from the account you bring, so include them as well. They just want to be sure you can access the funds in case of an emergency.

8. **Hidden issues:** Make sure to disclose anything that may not show up on your credit report, such as child support payments or income and alimony payments

or income. Lenders have ways of looking for things like this, so be upfront and disclose them, so nothing creeps up on you later. Also, if you make IRS payments or have a car under your brother's name but are making the payments yourself, please be clear and upfront about those as well. Your lender will look for patterns in your bank statements and any expenses that indicate such situations. Think of it this way, a loan officer may miss those small details, but an underwriter certainly won't.

9. **Work history:** Everyone needs a two-year work history. If you've had multiple employers over the past two years, be sure to bring start and end dates, addresses, and phone numbers as the lender will need to see any employment gaps. If there are gaps, you will have to go further back than two years to get the required work history. The best way to put it is to think as if you needed a resume for a job. A lender needs that resume. If the information you provide is inaccurate, there could be potential problems down the road. If you are a recent college grad, be sure to have your college dates, degree, and school transcripts, as you can use them for your work history and buy a home immediately after you start working. Also, don't fall for the misleading fact that you need two years with the same employer. That is not true. It is all right to have multiple employers as long as they are in the same industry. Many job changes will require an explanation and can cause denial as it shows unstable work history.

10. **Green cards and work permits:** If applicable, make sure to have your green card and work permit available, but be sure to check with your lender as some do not accept certain work permit categories. The work permit cannot be expired. If it is, bring proof of renewal receipt and previously expired permits to show proof of continuity.

The above is a general idea of the paperwork you may need to get a pre-approval. Having these handy and as complete as possible will help your lender get you a much faster pre-approval.

Once you have that pre-approval, you can start to look for a home. Remember, lenders have the traditional habit of issuing pre-approvals based on educated guesses. I simply cannot emphasize that enough.

Communicate and ask a lot of questions. A slightly better and more expensive home could carry a lesser payment than a cheaper home due to other expenses the home may carry, and you do not want to miss out on that opportunity simply because your pre-approval letter said so.

> Don't forget ... Price Doesn't Matter, Payment Does!!!

Chapter 6

The Dream Team

Nothing in life is as simple as it seems, especially the home buying process. There is so much that goes into buying a home, and most of the nightmares you hear about people having bad experiences are due to them not having the right professional team working for them. Choose wisely, and make sure they work well together.

The goal is, of course, to make sure that you have a team that is focused on getting you into a house. You need people who work well on an inter-agency level, and people who work well with you.

A mesh of personalities might not seem like much during a business deal, but there is a lot involved with purchasing a house, and you don't want to take the risk of any slights being given due to hurt feelings. A home buying deal can be made or broken based on the team you've put together. With that being said, let's take a look at the professionals along with their roles in helping you with your purchase.

The Right Team = A Successful Transaction

The Real Estate Professional: One of the biggest misunderstandings I see when it comes to hiring a real estate professional is thinking they are going to cost you a lot of money. That is absolutely not the case. When a seller hires a listing agent, a contract is arranged for a set fee and that fee gets split between the listing agent and the buyer's agent (your agent).

The seller is paying that fee regardless, even if you solely use the listing agent. The only difference is by utilizing the service of just the listing agent, he/she gets to keep the whole fee instead of splitting it. Remember, a listing agents' fiduciary responsibility is with the seller, not with you as the buyer. So, if it isn't costing you anything, why don't you make sure you have a good, knowledgeable agent to represent you?

An experienced real estate professional will definitely have all the contacts needed to get you started in the right direction.

I highly recommend you work with a realtor, which is not the same as a real estate agent. Realtors must abide a strict code of ethics as established by the NAR (National Association of Realtors), in addition to state requirements of continuing education. Realtors must take additional courses, training and tests on code of ethics. They also have access to additional resources and training that an average real estate agent does not have access to. Now, don't get me wrong. That is not to say good real estate agents have to be realtors, too. They don't, and there are plenty of good real estate agents out there, but it's important to know the difference between the two. All realtors are real estate agents but not all real estate agents are realtors, just like all CPAs are accountants, but not all accountants are CPAs.

The real estate professional you choose will help you find the right home, negotiate terms, set up inspections and, in some states, will even create the purchase and sales agreement. You will definitely be spending a lot of time with this person, so make sure you guys are a good fit for each other and that you get along.

The Lender: The lender you choose depends upon where you plan on getting your mortgage loan from. There are many options available. Let's take a look at 3 of the most common options below.

1. Local banks - Local banks are where you normally do your checking and savings banking. Local banks can have a lot of overlays at times, so ask questions if you plan on using them.
2. Mortgage brokers - Mortgage brokers do not lend money; they simply work as middlemen between you and the lender. The good thing about brokers is they have many options to choose from, and chances are they have access to lenders without overlays.
3. Correspondent non-delegated lenders - Similar to a broker, they have tons of options when it comes to lenders but in this case, they specifically lend their own money. This is pretty cool because, in addition to all their options, they control the transaction allowing for a faster clear to close.

With brokers or correspondent non-delegated, you have a ton more financing options, which give you the chance to shop around for the best deal.

Attorneys: There are usually three attorneys involved in a purchase transaction:

1. The Bank Attorney - The bank attorney represents the bank at the closing table. He / She is the bank attorney, but will often also represent the buyer (this is definitely not mandatory though, and you are always allowed to seek another attorney to represent you). In some cases, if you have an attorney who does bank work for other lenders, you can ask if the lender you are using will allow them to also do the closing. This is a good way to have your attorney do both, but it is not always allowed as some lenders do not take on new attorneys. Regardless of which way you go, always make sure to have an attorney represent you.
2. The Buyer's Attorney - The buyer's attorney represents the buyer in reviewing contracts such as the purchase and sales agreement. As mentioned above you can check and see if your attorney also does bank representation and see if your lender allows for new attorneys.
3. The Seller's Attorney - The seller's attorney represents the seller, and prepares the purchase and sales agreement in most cases.

Remember, contracts such as a purchase and sales agreement are usually prepared by the seller's attorney who has a responsibility to act in the seller's best interests, not yours. There is huge benefit in having an attorney looking out for your best interests while reviewing everything, and requesting changes on your behalf. Be sure to hire a good one because not all buyers' attorneys are good, and I have seen many drop the ball at the cost of a small fortune for their client.

Home Inspector: Once you have an accepted offer, it is extremely wise and prudent to get a home inspector. You can research to find one online, or your real estate professional can recommend a few if you'd prefer their help.

Some home inspectors do other types of inspections as well, such as pest inspections and radon inspections, so you can sometimes kill two birds with one stone if you plan on having other inspections to the property done. If you have multiple inspectors come out, make sure they are all certified in their areas of expertise.

*A website called Certified Master Inspector has a great list of home inspectors. https://certifiedmasterinspect-or.org/

Insurance Agent: You will need to get a homeowner's insurance policy for the home you are buying. Just like not being able to drive a new car off the dealership's lot without insurance, a lender will not allow you to close on a home unless there is insurance on the property. You may be able to bundle your homeowner's and auto insurance with your current carrier, but you can also definitely shop around for deals to find great coverage and lesser premiums.

Chapter 7
Your Dream Home Awaits

This is where the fun really begins! This part of the process can be exciting, but it can be frustrating at times, too, especially in a competitive sellers' market. The better prepared you are with what you are looking for, the easier the process. Let's jump in and go over what lies ahead.

Searching for the Right Home

This might be the step that everyone is most excited for, and often the one that takes the longest. Finding a home that fits your needs and budget is important. The first thing to do, of course, is to figure out exactly what you need. You need to think long-term. Make a list of everything that your house and property have to have.

We all have a vision of our dream home which may look like a five-bedroom house with three stories, four bathrooms, and an in-ground pool, but that's not financially feasible for everyone. On the flip, your family might need more than just a single bedroom house that easily fits within your budget or land equal to the size of a closet. Take your time with choosing your home. It's one decision you really want to get right.

Buying a house is a long-term investment, so think ahead. Will your family be expanding in the next five to ten years? Are pets in your future? If, for example, you are thinking about getting a dog or horse, you will want to look at the size of the yard and ascertain whether a fence or coverings will be needed.

Do you work from home? Will you need a smaller space to turn into an office or business room? You may not be purchasing your "forever home" right now but more than likely, you are going to stay for a while. These are the things that you are going to want to take into account.

Figure out where you want to live. Are you looking for a more rural or suburban feel? Do you want to stay in the same city, same county, or same state? All of these things will affect the search process, so be as detailed as possible.

Also, keep amenities in mind. Having an in-ground pool might not be the top priority for your purchase, but it's something to think about. Are you willing to pay extra for something like that if you do put it on your list of "wants"? If so, how much in price are you willing to go up? The simple things in life need to be considered for this far less simple decision. If there are other adults in the household, make sure to talk to them and see what their input is on the matter. If you are the sole decision maker involved in the move, it can be advised to discuss all of this with your real estate professional.

We often get caught up in the big picture. All the little, finer details can easily turn into a tangled knot. We're humans, and humans are forgetful beings, so having someone else to talk to and bounce ideas off of just might be the final thing you need to figure out what's missing from your house-hunting search.

Again, I cannot stress enough how important it is to make lists. Keep track of every idea and make sure to note down every possibility.

Moving is a lot of work filled with time-consuming details. Those details are important, though, even if they might not seem to be that big of a deal. You are about to take on a change and make a choice that will literally alter the path of your current life. Don't rush! Think things through!

Make sure that you are able to work things out, especially at this phase in the game. So far, you haven't made any commitments. You are still looking for the house in question, which means everything is just sort of soft-locked into place.

Some people want to take the strait-laced route and only look at the houses they know are going to fit into their mold. Other people might be a little flexible in their decisions and consider looking at houses they might not have picked on their own, houses that are a little more expensive than they originally considered, or houses with other amenities than what was originally decided upon.

The way that you handle this part of the home picking process is all up to you. Right now, there's no right or wrong decision to be made. Explore and find the path and the house that fits your unique needs.

Another thing to note when making up the game plan for your property is that you should look at your prospective homes personally. That's going to cost time and gas money, so you may want to streamline the process. Check to see if any of the homes you are looking at have virtual tours you can walk through to see if it's worth making the trip. Try to view several homes on the same day to save time or visit several homes in the same area.

In fact, it helps to make sure that you are able to have a candid conversation about the situation with your real estate professional. Let them know exactly what you are looking for. You don't have to be worried about being too specific. It's their job to help locate houses you are interested in.

Things will go a lot smoother if you are able to be open and honest about what you are looking for. Let your real estate professional help cut down on some of the fancy footwork.

It might sound fun to try and tackle this as a solo pay-as-you-go process, but considering the seller is the one paying your agent's fee for you, make sure to take advantage. Honestly, they're some of the most helpful members of your team!

Bidding Wars and Negotiating an Offer

There is no doubt that we are currently in a crazy sellers' market. Competitive is an understatement. Here is a little inside info on submitting an offer, and some strategies that may help you. For information on the market in the area you live in and how to proceed with an offer, there's no one to better advise you than your local, excellent real estate professional but here are just a few pointers for you anyway:

When buying a home, you most often have a down payment and closing costs. Sometimes buyers have the down payment but don't have the required funds for the closing costs, so they try to negotiate the closing costs as a seller credit as part of the offer. This happens a lot, but in a competitive market, the more you request from a seller, the less likely you'll be at successfully getting a property that has multiple offers on it because you are basically asking the seller to give you money out of their proceeds to cover some of your expenses. In a multiple offer situation, they will most definitely go with an offer that puts more money in their pocket. Therefore, if you are able to save a little more money to cover some, or all, of your closing costs, your chances of an accepted offer will exponentially increase. Using your own funds makes you appear as a strong buyer.

Generally, when you submit an offer, you usually put down two deposits (depending on the area that you live in). The first deposit is a good faith deposit and is provided with the initial offer to secure the property while you conduct inspections, and so on. This is usually a small deposit. The second, much larger deposit is given when you sign the purchase and sales agreement, which once fully executed, supersedes the offer.

A smaller initial deposit, which is often $500-$1000, makes it fairly easy for buyers to walk away from the deal if they change their mind. Putting in a larger first deposit is a great strategy to make your offer more appealing to a seller, as you'd be more locked in, and likely less apt to walk away. Not many people care about $500, but if you were on the hook for $3,000, that might be a different story. If you do put down a larger deposit, be sure that this is the home for you. If you change your mind and walk away, you will lose those funds. In the end, the best thing to remember is that the more money you put down for first and second deposits, the more appealing your offer will be to the seller.

Another competitive strategy to use is a waiver of a home inspection. This is definitely not my favorite option, and I am personally against a buyer waiving a home inspection, but I do see this occur often. Waiving the home inspection contingency pretty much means you are buying a home without really knowing what condition it may be in. This can be risky, but sellers love not having to worry about a home inspection, so doing this can definitely put you closer to the front of the line in a bidding war.

You can also consider creating an agreement to do a home inspection for informational purposes only, would allow you to do the home inspection and know the condition of the property, but exclude you from using that inspection as a negotiating tool. Just be aware that if you back out, you could lose that first deposit depending on the terms of your agreement.

Another method used to outbid competition in a bidding war is an escalation clause. An escalation clause allows buyers the opportunity to escalate or increase their offer up to a maximum specified amount to beat out the competing offers. This action gets triggered when an offer is received that is higher than the one the buyers in question initially submitted.

So, let's say you are looking at a home for sale at $400,000, and there are multiple offers on the table. You offer $430,000 with a $1,000 escalation clause up to a maximum of $450,000. If there is another offer on the table for $435,000, your offer will automatically increase to $436,000. This can help tremendously. You will usually request evidence of the other offer before fully committing.

Here is another tactic you can use in the bidding process. Let's say you see a property listed at $400,000 with another multiple offer situation. You can offer a ridiculously high number like $480,000 (even though you know the property is not worth it) but make the offer subject to a property appraisal coming in at or above purchase price. One of two things will happen in a situation like this if your offer gets accepted.

First, if the house is appraised at or above the $480,000, congrats, you would get the house for what it's worth! If the house appraises at a lower price, $450,000 for example you would go back to the seller for negotiations to drop the price. Although a seller is not forced to drop the price, most of the time they will. I've seen this work many times with inexperienced listing agents who get blindsided by a higher number and think that's the stronger offer, but a seasoned agent will look much deeper into the strengths of what is actually being presented.

A different technique that many sellers love is this one, and it could work for you. Simply waive the appraisal contingency if you have a little bit of money to burn, and want the house badly enough. Basically, if we use the same example above where you submit an offer of $480,000 on a property listed at $400,000 and the appraisal comes in at $450,000, you would pay the extra $30,000 to the seller. This ensures them that they are getting their money regardless.

Here's one last approach to use during the bidding process. It's an oldie and has worked many times, but I usually only see it work when there is an emotional attachment to the property. Write a letter to the seller listing your reasons for wanting to buy the home, and tell them a little about yourself. I recently encountered a home that was custom built in the 1960s for a couple and their two children. The children, all grown up now and out of the house with their own families, were selling the home because the parents had passed on. With a multiple offer situation, the children didn't pick the best or the strongest offer. Instead, they ended up picking the only one submitted with a letter. The letter described a beautiful family and enthusiastically explained why they wanted the home. The sellers' emotional attachment to the home made them care more about a good family getting the property than the dollar amount of available offers. Sometimes a listing agent will put a little info about the property history in the public description to help you identify a property like this, but trust me, this will work in only specific circumstances, and not work for the guy flipping a house who is all about his bottom line.

There are many ways to get creative with an offer to get you to compete in a bidding war and increase your chances of winning the property, and I have many more up my sleeve but always keep in mind that no one can better help you than the real estate professional you have chosen.

Important Offer Dates

A lot of real estate professionals do a horrible job at properly explaining an offer's important dates and consequences. A good friend of mine in North Carolina just lost $2,000, and had no idea that money was at risk due to the failure of the agent properly explaining the offer.

For some of these dates, it is the lender that needs to hit the deadlines, so you want to make sure you have an agent that stays on top of what is required. It is so important to work with a team of professionals that all work well together and communicate. Let's take a look at a few of these dates below.

Mortgage Contingency Date: Other than the closing date, this is the most important deadline. I always like to see this date no more than 7 days prior to the closing date. This is the date in which all financing must be in order and complete.

That means that there are no outstanding items and that the lender is now committed to giving you the loan. That also means there is a clean title and good appraisal report. If you are unable to get all financing ready for this date, you **MUST** be sure to request an **EXTENSION** of that date.

This is the date when all of your deposits are released to the seller, and there is definitely no going back. You either close or you lose all of your money. If you have a good attorney representing you, a clause would be added in to limit the damages in case this happens. Without this clause all of your money could be at risk. **DO NOT** rely on anyone to keep on track of these dates for you. I see professionals drop the ball all the time, putting buyers' funds at risk.

There is a good reason why I personally like to see this date be set for no more than seven days prior to closing. Final verifications on a mortgage have to be done less than ten days prior to close. Let's say you get a commitment 15 days prior to closing, and your deposit is released to the seller. Then, you enter the period of those ten days, and something crept up on your credit report, changing your qualification. Do you know what could happen? Well, guess what?! If your commitment letter was given and the change disqualifies you from getting the mortgage, you would lose your deposit. We can talk all day about the reasons and things that can happen which can cause you to lose your deposit, but what I want embedded into your mind is that the closer to the closing date your commitment is, the safer your money will be.

Here is a good example of something that happened to someone I know that was caused by a lack of communication on the team's part, and a lack of knowledge and understanding on the buyer's part. The commitment letter was due, and financing was not yet finalized. If I have taught you anything yet, it is that if financing is not 100% complete, you **MUST** get an extension on the commitment date or you can lose money. In this case, the buyer's attorney sent the buyer a mortgage commitment extension to sign, extending the mortgage commitment by a week. Since the mortgage commitment was being extended, the closing date needed extension as well. The buyer signed the extensions, and the buyer's attorney sent it to the seller's attorney.

Now, what occurred was the buyer's real estate agent also sent the buyer an extension to sign but did not extend the mortgage commitment. The agent missed that completely and sent an extension only for the closing date, keeping the mortgage commitment date the same. The buyer signed that extension, and the agent forwarded it to the seller's attorney as well.

Guess what happened?!

The seller's attorney now had two extensions, both executed by the buyer, and the only thing left to make either one official was the seller's signature. Well, the seller's attorney chose the one extending only the closing date, therefore releasing the buyer's deposit to the sellers.

The buyers had $15,000 on the hook, and the seller's attorney was super clear that if that deal did not close on time, they had every intention of keeping the deposit and relisting the property. Fortunately, the buyer closed on time, but can you just imagine the stress level one goes through in a situation like this? Scenarios like this can be avoided with the help of an experienced agent, and some buyer knowledge. I have decided to put my 18 years of experience into this book to help buyers have more successful transactions to help them avoid situations like this.

Closing Date: This is the day you sign your life away and get the keys to your new home. The most important thing to know about this date is to make sure you get an extension if unable to close on time. Extensions are quite common and happen all the time.

Inspection Dates: When you submit an offer, you have a limited amount of time to conduct and respond to any inspections. Usually, you have 7 to 10 days to conduct an inspection, and 24 to 72 hours to respond to the seller on the results of those inspections. If you need more time, you must ask for that time in writing for an extension. Failing to extend could cause you to lose your rights to the inspection and waive that contingency.

Purchase and Sales Date: This is the deadline to have a fully executed purchase and sales agreement. Depending on what part of the country you are in, this can vary. Some places go directly into a purchase and sales agreement right away, while in other areas, you usually jump into a purchase and sales after inspections are done, just in case there are any changes or negotiations due to those inspections.

Things in real estate can differ from location to location, so it is always good to have someone well-versed in your area. In Massachusetts, a fully-executed purchase and sales are usually expected within 14 days, but none of these dates are concrete and can change depending on the situation and the offer submitted.

Mortgage Application Date: This is the date that you are expected to have a complete mortgage application submitted by. Usually, this is between 7 to 14 days but again, this could change from area to area and depends on the offer submitted.

Offer Duration Date: This is how long your offer is valid, and the time frame the seller has to sign and accept your offer in order for it to be valid and fully executed. Once the date passes, your offer is no longer valid, and you are not committed to that deal anymore. That date is usually 24 hours, but on listings where they are expecting multiple offers, the offer duration date could be a few days.

Home and Other Inspections

When buying a home, you have a series of available inspections you can conduct on the property, and the ones you do will definitely vary.

The real estate professional helping you should be able to guide you on these inspections. Some of the inspections you may conduct on a home are, but are not limited to, a home inspection of the overall condition of the property, lead paint inspection, radon test and inspection, and pest inspection.

Negotiating Inspection Results

Some people completely misunderstand the purpose of a home inspection. The purpose of a home inspection is to understand the condition of the property and to address major concerns. I once saw a buyer request the seller finish an unfinished basement, not because of a home inspection but because he wanted a finished basement. That is not really the point. A home inspection gives you the opportunity to address major issues such as plumbing, heating, electrical, structural or roof issues. You can negotiate a price reduction or a seller credit to assist with closing costs, or you can simply have the seller fix it if he is willing and able to.

A seller may not have the funds to fix the items requested, so that's when you can ask for a price reduction or a seller credit to help pay for your closing costs so you can have more funds available to fix the issue yourself. You can also ask for smaller issues to be addressed and fixed or to get a credit or price reduction, but inspections aren't really meant to nitpick at every little issue.

As you know, most homes you buy won't be perfect unless it's a new construction (and even then, it's not perfect). Also, remember that it's a sellers' market, and requesting too much could push for the seller to cancel the deal and go with another buyer. I recently saw a buyer try to ask a seller for too many small and tedious fixes, and the seller didn't even try to negotiate.

They simply dropped the buyer and went with another of the several offers they had. The buyer then tried to tell the seller to forget it and that they would do the repairs themselves, but the seller didn't care and, out of frustration, selected a different buyer.

The Purchase and Sales Agreement

The purchase and sales agreement in most places comes right after the home inspection. Price reductions and/or seller credits will be reflected in the purchase and sales agreement. Or, if the seller agrees to do repairs, a repair addendum is then added to the purchase and sales agreement.

Now, not everyone will produce an offer and then create a purchase and sales agreement. Some go directly into a purchase and sales agreement, and then renegotiate the agreement (which ends up being the same thing). The purchase and sales agreement is important because most appraisers won't even go to look at a property or do an appraisal without knowing the terms of the agreement. So, the sooner you can get through the home inspection and get everything negotiated to jump into a purchase and sales agreement, the better and faster the process will go.

Chapter 8

Securing Financing

The initial pre-approval is established by a loan officer, and is rarely reviewed by an underwriter. Even when it is reviewed by an underwriter, when you arrive at the time to secure financing, there will be updating to do and additional documents to submit.

Securing your financing comes as soon as you find a property and have a signed purchase and sales agreement. Let us jump in and look at what can be expected.

Required Documents

The documents you will need once you start to secure your financing are pretty much all the same documents as your pre-approval, but you may need a few additional ones, too. If more than 30 days have lapsed since you got your pre-approval, be sure to bring all updated documents such as pay stubs, bank statements, profit and loss statements if self-employed, and so on.

Some additional documents you will see a lender typically ask for are copies of the cashed deposit checks you gave for the initial deposit, the purchase and sales agreement (an updated bank statement will have to be provided to show these cashed checks), a letter of explanation for inquiries on your credit report (they just want to be sure you do not have any additional liability they didn't know about), letters of explanation for things such as addresses showing on your credit report but not on the credit application, gaps of employment, and reasons for purchasing another owner-occupied investment property if you already own one.

You will also need to submit gift letters and your relationship to the person gifting you funds if you're getting a monetary gift, as well as their bank statement.

It is impossible to put everything a lender can ask for into a book, so you just need to remember one thing: work with an experienced professional! Everyone has a unique situation, and an experienced loan officer will catch many things an underwriter will ask for.

At this stage, your file gets sent to an underwriter for a real approval (no longer a pre-approval) Once received, you will be provided with a list of documents needed, such as the ones mentioned earlier. Keep in mind that, some documents you submit may trigger the underwriter to ask for more and more documentation. For example, if you made a large deposit into your bank account after your pre-approval, you will need to provide solid evidence of where that large deposit came from. The lender will want to source it, and a letter from your mother stating she gave you the cash would not suffice.

Also, if you have any type of child support or alimony payments, make sure to have your divorce decree and other court documents, as the lender will need them. As with any other document required on a loan, you must provide all pages.

Motivation Letters and Letters of Explanation

This is really important. Depending on your transaction, you will need to provide motivation letters or letters of explanation for certain things. This is important because people tend to forget that an underwriter, who is also a human being, is reviewing your file. The letters you send must make sense, be convincing, and provide the appropriate information.

When I was an underwriter, I didn't like when a buyer would try to pull a fast one on me. I would see this often and end up denying the file. For example, if you are buying a three-family owner-occupied building but already own one, you need a strong motivational letter.

Here is an example of a weak motivational letter that was denied by an underwriter:

> "The main reasons why we want another building are because we currently have three bedrooms, and the new house has four. We have three kids and need more space. The new house also has a three-car garage that's nice, and we don't have a garage."

The above letter was denied as the underwriter didn't feel that the buyer included sufficient reason, and felt more like the buyer was simply buying another investment property.

On the other hand, the letter below was approved because it gave adequate justification. Take a look:

> "There are a couple of good reasons why we are looking to purchase another multifamily building. First, my wife and I have three children, all girls, of which the younger two currently share a room. They are 8 years old, 11 years old, and 17 years old. The bedroom is small, which is causing the girls to constantly fight over their personal belongings. The constant bickering is causing a lot of stress in our household, and we need to give each of the girls their own room. The new home has four bedrooms, which is a huge upgrade from our three bedrooms and could give us that peace of mind. Another reason we are very interested in this new building is that it has a three-car garage. It's very rare to see a three-family home with garages. Our current parking situation at our current home is OK in the summer, but in the winter, it is an absolute nightmare. Between getting the kids ready for school, scraping ice off the vehicles, clearing the snow, and shoveling, it is just simply overwhelming at times. The three-car garage will give us more free time as we wouldn't have to deal with cleaning the vehicles.
>
> Thank you very much in advance for your consideration."

I'm sure you can see why one was approved over the other. Tell your story and give good reasons for your purchase. These underwriters don't know you from a hole in the wall. They only see the letters you provide.

Now, let's discuss letters of explanation. Some letters require more explanations than others. You may need letters explaining a credit inquiry just as well as a letter for gaps in employment. Only provide the necessary info, and avoid being verbose.

For example, I saw someone give way too much information on a credit inquiry letter. The bank asked about an inquiry for a $10,000 credit card that the buyer obtained almost 4 months ago, which was already reporting an $8,000 balance on the credit report.

A simple letter stating that the card was obtained and is now showing on the credit report would have been sufficient, but instead, the buyer went on to tell his whole life story. In the letter, he stated that he got the credit card to get $5,000 cash out to buy the house. He pretty much opened Pandora's Box because, as you'll remember from earlier in the book, you cannot borrow money and apply those funds to the purchase of a home.

You see, banks only require two months of bank statements, and he deposited the $5,000 from the credit card just a hair over three months ago, so it was irrelevant at that time. Since the bank didn't see it, the bank didn't care but now he openly admitted to getting the card to borrow money. Long story short, he now had $5,000 less to purchase the home with and could not complete the purchase because the lender would not allow the use of those borrowed funds. Be concise and minimal when writing letters of explanation.

Getting Insurance

Getting insurance on a property you are buying is mandatory before you close, and is no different than getting car insurance on a car before you leave the car dealership. Be sure to start shopping for insurance as soon as possible, and get the policy information in to the lender to ensure the process flows smoothly.

You have the right to choose any insurance company you want, but most people start with the agency that holds their car insurance policy. Be sure to ask the lender for the "mortgagee clause" which is a provisional clause used between the mortgage lender and the insurance provider. You will provide this clause to your insurance agent, and then your agent will create the insurance binder the lender will need with this clause listed.

The Appraisal

Here is a fun fact, just because you qualify for a mortgage does not mean the property will. An appraisal report is not just about value; it is also about property condition. The lender has the right to deny a loan if they do not like the collateral. This is important to know. If you are purchasing a foreclosure or short sale, the condition of the property is very important to the lender as most foreclosures or short sales are in rough shape.

This is another reason why it is so important to work with an experienced real estate professional and loan officer.

You want to avoid attempting to buy a home that the lender wouldn't ever approve if the home you are looking at requires a rehab loan instead of a conventional or FHA.

Once you get to this point, and the lender has the purchase and sales agreement, they will order the appraisal report. Once the appraisal report comes in, the lender should give you a copy. This report is for your eyes and the lender's eyes only. You do not have to share the information on this report unless you need to renegotiate the price due to low value or if the property needs some sort of repair for the lender to accept the collateral.

I once saw a buyer share the information of the report, and they were buying the house for far less than what it was worth. The seller found out, and as a result, pulled out of the deal to try and get more money for the house since they now knew what it was worth. Of course, you could go after them and try to force them to sell, but to some people, it may not be worth the hassle. So again, once the appraisal report comes in, it is for your eyes only.

The Wait

For a good part of this process, you will be mostly waiting. While you are waiting, the attorneys and lender will finish up a bunch of internal items. One of those items is the title, for example.

The attorney will conduct a title search to be sure you get a clean title, and if there are any encumbrances, they will work on getting them cleared. Title is just a small piece of all the internal things going on while you wait. Follow up from time to time to make sure nothing else is needed from you in the meantime.

> **Tip:** If you are renting an apartment do not turn it in until you have 100% certainty that you are closing. Most people sometimes don't realize that a closing can fall apart just as much on the sellers' side as it can on the buyer's side. Sometimes you may even end up paying an extra month of rent. Paying an extra month of rent will be much better than ending up homeless as I have seen this happen a good handful of times.

Chapter 9

Cleared to Close & The Closing

Nothing is more exciting as you get closer to your closing date. It can be nerve-racking because sometimes, people are rushing to get last-minute things and documents in to finalize the deal. Sellers are packing, the buyer is packing, and it can simply get crazy at times. Then, you get that phone call, and the lender tells you that you are CTC. So, what does that mean?! Let's jump in and see.

CTC "Music to My Ears"

CTC is an acronym for "cleared to close." This means the lender has completed all tasks and has authorized you to close. This is literally music to my ears! There are a few things to keep in mind that most people do not realize.

Just because a lender says you are cleared to close does not mean the deal cannot fall apart before you sign on the dotted line. If you quit your job, for example, before closing, or purchase new furniture or a new car thinking everything is all set, well, I have news for you, and it might not be good. Any changes to your credit or financial situation even after a clear to close could disqualify you, i.e., if your debt-to-income ratio changes significantly.

Also, if the lender finds out, which I am pretty darn sure they will, you could lose your clear to close and possibly even your deposits at that point. It is so important that during the process, up until you actually get the keys to your new home, you do not make any changes at all ... like absolutely ZERO changes.

Keep everything the same. Do not quit your job because your boss is hard to deal with or anything of the sort. I have seen people make it all the way to the finish line and royally screw things up for themselves and not be able to close. So, once you get that CTC, do not move a muscle until you have signed all closing docs and have your keys in your hands.

The Closing

This is the moment you have been anxiously waiting for. Here is what usually happens and what to expect. A few days before the closing, you will be notified of the amount of funds you are required to bring with you to the closing table. Again, this will happen at least a few days prior. Usually, those funds are to be submitted by certified check. As technology has advanced, so has the streamlining of many of the procedures involved in real estate transactions. One such procedure is the use of wire transfers to submit funds. In my opinion, you should use caution when it comes to wire transfers. There has been a lot of hacking into email systems. I actually had a couple of experiences where my buyers got an email from the attorney stating to wire the closing money. My buyers contacted me out of confusion to check and see if this was accurate. Thank God they did because the emails looked 100% legit and had all the right numbers. The only thing was that it was not sent by the attorney. It was a hack trying to steal the buyer's money. I'm not sure how these hackers get the information to attempt this scam, but as I have seen it with my own eyes, I recommend you be very careful when asked to wire funds.

Chances are you will go to the bank and get a certified check the morning of or the day before closing. Prior to meeting the closing attorney, you will have to do a final walk-through of the home to ensure it is in the exact condition discussed, and that things promised were done either the day before or the morning of closing.

Personally, I always suggest going to view the home on the morning of the closing. I once saw a buyer who viewed a home the night before then went to sign docs in the morning. When she arrived at her new home and went to turn the water on, nothing came out. Upon inspection, she found out that someone went in during the night and ripped out all of the copper pipes.

What a mess but now she owned that mess, and when asked at the closing table if she viewed the home and if everything was OK prior to signing, she was clueless as to what happened during the night. In other words, she was stuck with the problem. Therefore, I always suggest a final morning walkthrough.

After you get the check and ensure the property is OK, you are ready to sign your life away. Congrats! You are now a proud homeowner! 😊

Chapter 10

Post-Closing

This is awesome! You are officially a homeowner, but that doesn't mean you are out of the woods just yet. There is a lot that goes into owning a home.

Below are some tips and pointers to help you on your new journey.

Utilities

Make sure to quickly get utilities transferred into your name as soon as possible. Call the electric or gas company right away, and do not drop the ball on this.

I knew a buyer that didn't have power for two entire weeks because he dropped the ball and didn't call the power company.

In case you are wondering who, that buyer was ... well, it was me! I was so busy I totally forgot to get the power switched over, and there you have it. I had no power for two whole weeks.

Check Your Windows

Believe it or not, 25% to 30% of heat loss is through your windows, but it does not have to be that way. Weatherstripping is a simple and cost-effective solution, so make sure to check for drafts and then head to a local hardware store, like Home Depot or Lowes.

Outdoor Water Faucets and Hoses

If you live in an area with cold weather, as I do, make sure to shut the water valve to outdoor faucets and disconnect water hoses before the temperatures drop.

This is to prevent any pipes from freezing and bursting. You can turn it all back on again in the spring.

Look for Cracks

It's a good idea to walk around the house's exterior and look for cracks in the walkway, driveway, and even the foundation.

Once you spot them, fill the cracks to avoid water from getting in and freezing in the winter. Water expands when it freezes, so little by little, as it gets into these cracks, freezes, and expands, it can make a small problem bigger over time.

Filters and Heating

If you have an HVAC heating or cooling system, make sure you have quality, clean filters. Clogged filters can cost you money.

It is also a good idea to look for a local company to give your heating system, regardless if it's oil, gas, or propane, an annual cleaning to keep it running efficiently. These systems can last a lifetime if properly maintained.

Flashlights & Batteries

It is always a great idea to always keep extra batteries in the house for flashlights, fire alarms, or any other emergency uses. You can never go wrong with being prepared.

Don't Ignore the Leaves

Once fall hits, be sure to rake up all the leaves. When they get wet, they can suffocate the grass and lead to all kinds of insect and disease problems. Plus, who wants a yard full of leaves instead of beautiful green grass?

Check for Water Leaks

This is huge. You will have to pay the town for water and sewer unless you have a private well and sewer, which can get expensive if you have an unknown leak somewhere.

It is good to check the toilets to make sure they are not constantly running and to check the interior and exterior faucets for drips. This can save you a lot of money in the long run.

Your Fixed Payment Isn't So Fixed

Most likely, you got yourself a fixed mortgage rate, but within the first to second year of homeownership, you may see a change in your mortgage payment due to escrows. Generally, you will get a letter titled "Escrow Shortage".

This occurs when taxes and insurance are included as part of your payment. So, while your principal and interest are fixed for 30 years, your taxes and insurance are not. They depend entirely on the city or town you live in, as well as the insurance company you selected for your homeowner's insurance policy. Due to this, you will see a change in your payment from time to time as the lender makes adjustments to keep up with those payments. It happens to everyone, so do not freak out if you see a change. It does not mean you don't have a fixed rate if that is what you chose.

A Closing Note

> Thank you for taking the time to invest in this guide and by doing so, investing in yourself and your home buying future. I hope you finish this book and begin an inspired and exciting future in home buying. I just wanted to close by wishing you the best and reminding you one last time: Price doesn't matter, Payment does!
>
> *-Julio C Roque*